```
92        Lakin, Pat.
CAP           Jennifer
            Capriati
```

FEB 17 2004 | DATE DUE |

$13.00

MEMORIAL SCHOOL LIBRARY
UNION BEACH, NJ 07735

```
Jennifer Capriati /
92 CAP                    1311151
Lakin, Pat.
    MEMORIAL SCHOOL LIBRARY
```

# Jennifer Capriati

*Rising Star*

**Patricia Lakin**

ROURKE ENTERPRISES, INC.
VERO BEACH, FLORIDA 32964

© 1993 Rourke Enterprises, Inc.

All rights reserved. No part of this book may be reproduced or utilized in any form or by any means, electronic or mechanical including photocopying, recording, or by any information storage and retrieval system without permission in writing from the publisher.

A Blackbirch Graphics Book.

### Library of Congress Cataloging-in-Publication Data

Lakin, Pat.
    Jennifer Capriati / by Patricia Lakin.
      p.   cm. — (The Winning spirit)
    Includes index.
    Summary: Traces the life of the young woman who entered professional tennis at the age of thirteen and won a gold medal in the 1992 Olympics.
    ISBN 0-86592-090-7
    1. Capriati, Jennifer—Juvenile literature. 2. Tennis players—United States—Biography—Juvenile literature. [1. Capriati, Jennifer. 2. Tennis players.] I. Title. II. Series.
GV994.C36L35   1993
796.342′092—dc20
[B]
                                        93-18131
                                               CIP
                                                 AC

# *Contents*

**1** At the 1992 Olympics  5

**2** Born with a Racket  13

**3** Bring on the Coach  18

**4** Turning Pro  27

**5** Star-Spangled Summer  37

Glossary  46

For Further Reading  46

Index  47

# 1

# At the 1992 Olympics

*"I have my ups and downs like everybody else."*

Sixteen-year-old Jennifer arrived in Barcelona, Spain, the city where the 1992 Summer Olympics were to be played.

Was she a typical American tourist, there to watch world-famous athletes compete for their countries?

Not quite. Jennifer *was* one of those world-famous athletes. Her full name is Jennifer Capriati, and she went to the Olympics to represent the United States in tennis.

Even though Jennifer is just a teenager, she is tall—five feet seven inches—and powerful. She is the youngest female in U.S. history to become a professional tennis player. At 14, she reached the semifinals at Wimbledon, a world-famous tennis tournament held each year in

*Opposite: As one of the youngest top players in professional tennis, Jennifer has amazed the world with her talent. Here, she celebrates her victory over Martina Navratilova in the semifinals at Wimbledon in 1991.*

England. By the young age of 15, Jennifer had defeated Martina Navratilova and Gabriela Sabatini, two of the world's top tennis players. And, at 16, she became the youngest American ever to win the Olympic gold medal in tennis.

## A Pressured Time

As she prepared for the Olympics, Jennifer might not have been thinking about the positive accomplishments of her life. Not only was she nervous about representing her country, but she was also concerned about her recent losses. She had suffered a quarterfinal loss to Gabriela Sabatini at the Australian Open and lost her first match at the Pan Pacific Open in Tokyo. It was now August, and Jennifer hadn't won a single title so far in 1992.

In between the Australian Open and Pan Pacific Tour, Jennifer didn't have time to return home to Florida, school, and her friends. She has always taken tennis and her school work very seriously. So, she continued with her tennis playing, her training, and her school assignments. Jennifer worked three hours each day with a tutor to keep up with her tenth-grade class at the Palmer Academy. There was the added pressure of a chemistry midterm to study for. This was a lot of pressure for just one person to take, considering that Jennifer is also a normal teenager going through the tough changes that the teen years bring.

Jennifer went through some tough losses in 1992 but, with the support and advice of her family, friends, and coaches, she was able to make a great comeback.

Unlike most girls her age, Jennifer suffers those pressures under the critical eye of the press. Some reporters were especially hard on Jennifer after she cut her Japan trip short, packed up her rackets, and headed home to Saddlebrook, Florida.

News reporters asked, "Is tennis superstar Jennifer Capriati burned out?"

## Jennifer Answers the Press

Jennifer responded, "Everybody likes you when you win, but when you lose, they have to think up things that aren't true. I wonder how they'd like it if someone wrote something hurtful like that about their family?"

She went on to say, "Everyone thinks I have it so great and that this is such an easy life, but it's not true either. Besides dealing with tennis, I'm dealing with all this adolescence stuff. I have my ups and downs like anybody else. It's normal. And most of it is nobody's business but mine."

Jennifer then cleared the air about whether she might want to leave tennis. "Just because I take five weeks off to concentrate on school, that means I'm burned out? Get real. Let's say that some day I decided I do hate tennis and I want to quit, well then I'm going to need my school. And if I like being at home with my friends and getting away from the tennis, what's wrong with that?"

## *A Strong Foundation*
World-famous tennis pro and longtime friend, Chris Evert, was obviously proud of Jennifer's comments. "You have to give her credit for asking these questions and confronting these issues at a young age," she said. "There's a silver lining there."

Chris Evert is probably right. And the silver lining just might be Jennifer's strong emotional base. She has a devoted and loving family. Her mom, Denise, and dad, Stefano, and her younger brother, Steven, all help to keep her life balanced. Jennifer would probably add her dog, Bianca, to the family group. Chris Evert, however, is someone who can sympathize with Jennifer in a way no one else can.

Chris met Jennifer when Jennifer was a little girl. Chris's dad, Jimmy Evert, was Jennifer's first professional coach. Chris saw Jennifer develop from raw talent to a real tennis pro. She offered Jennifer guidance and friendship. One gift she gave Jennifer many Christmases ago says it all: a gold bracelet engraved with the message "Love, Chris." Jennifer never takes the bracelet off.

Besides all of this support from family and friends, Jennifer did have some success after her Tokyo defeat in February 1992. She was pitted against Monica Seles, the number one player in the world in March of 1992. They were competing in the Lipton International

*Jennifer is a remarkably focused person for someone her age. Her ability to concentrate on her goals is one of the keys to her success.*

Players Championships in Key Biscayne, Florida. Jennifer played brilliantly and broke Monica's 27-match winning streak.

Jennifer described what went through her head during the game. "After I won the first set, I kept saying to myself to pretend that the second set was the first set. I kept saying she's [Monica] probably going to come out fighting now, but I didn't let her take control as much as she always does. I served a lot better."

Monica commented after the match, "Physically, she's very strong. She was making it hard for me to play great on every point. She definitely played a lot better than I did. I was just playing to stay in the match, not to win it."

And finally, Jennifer's new coach, Pavel Slozil, talked about Jennifer's time off from tennis. "She had to regroup." He added, "She's got guts. I knew she had something excellent; that's why I came to work with her."

## Getting Ready

Another coach, Tom Gullikson also praises Jennifer. According to him, "Jennifer is the most talented player we've ever had in this country; there's no doubt in my mind about that. But no player her age has had to deal with the burden of so many other people's expectations. She can be number one if she wants to and for as long as she wants to, but to do it, she has to commit to tennis...."

Jennifer agrees. "When you're thirteen, it's no big deal to say you want to be number one. But it is a big deal to actually get there."

And it's not just training harder or playing longer. After Tokyo, Jennifer realized that she needed to make some changes. She worked on a program to turn her tennis around. The first thing she focused on was a better diet. She cut way back on eating sweets. Jennifer won her battle. Before going to Barcelona and the Olympics, she had lost 20 pounds. "I have to say that losing weight made a lot of difference. It brought out my confidence."

And Jennifer turned to an old family friend for help with her game. Manuel Santana was the 1966 Wimbeldon winner. He practiced with Jennifer in preparation for the Olympics.

But with such an unsettling past few months, could Jennifer meet the challenge?

# 2

# Born with a Racket

*"The day Jennifer was born, Stefano said he was going to make her a tennis player."*

Even though Jennifer Capriati is one of the youngest tennis stars, she has been playing tennis for at least 13 years. Was she born with a racket in her hand? Not exactly. But it was obvious from an early age that Jennifer would be some kind of athlete. In order to understand Jennifer's interest and determination in this sport, it is important to learn something about her parents and her early life.

## Jennifer's Parents

Denise, Jennifer's mother, was a flight attendant based in New York. On one of her European trips, she had a few days off in Torremolinos, Spain. She decided to relax by the hotel pool.

That simple choice was an important decision. It was beside that hotel pool where she and her future husband, Stefano, met. He was a dark-haired, good-looking athletic man. He was swimming in the pool when he looked up. Denise and Stefano spotted one another. They were instantly attracted.

Although born and raised in Italy, Stefano was working in Spain as a stunt man. He had also played soccer in Italy, but a knee injury had put an end to that.

To this day, Stefano Capriati does not like to talk about that part of his life. Perhaps the injury left scars of disappointment. He moved to Spain and turned to another career...the athletically demanding work of a stunt man. He appeared in the American films, *100 Rifles*, *Patton*, and *The Last Run*.

Stefano and Denise dated for two years and married in 1974 on Christmas Day. They made their first home in Spain.

## A Family of Tennis Lovers

When Stefano first arrived in Spain, he began to play tennis. Once he and Denise were married, Denise learned the game and loved it as much as Stefano did. When Denise became pregnant with their first child, Jennifer, she continued to play tennis and to jog.

Denise and Stefano wanted their child to be American, so they moved to New York, close to where Denise had grown up. On March 29, 1976, only 17 hours after playing a game of tennis, Denise gave birth to Jennifer.

There is nothing ordinary about Jennifer Capriati. And she entered the world that way, too. Most infants weigh anywhere from 6 to 9 pounds at birth. Jennifer weighed 11!

"The day Jennifer was born, Stefano said he was going to make her a tennis player," Denise recalls. "He actually said it before she was born. He just knew it from the way I was built and the way I carried."

## *The Proper Body*

Was Stefano someone who could predict the future? Not really. With regard to becoming a tennis player, he says, "You must be born with the proper body, but then you have to use that body properly."

Jennifer proved at a very young age that she not only had the body but the ability as well.

Denise recalls an early sign of Jennifer's unusual athletic ability. It occurred in Spain in a playground. "Jennifer couldn't have been more than nine months old, when I saw her climbing up the monkey bars. She couldn't even walk, but she was so strong that she would crawl up to the bars and start climbing them. When she'd get to the top, the other mothers in the playground would say, 'Aren't you scared? Look where Jennifer is?' And I'd

*When Jennifer was just two or three months old, her father started to prepare her to be a professional athlete. With her father's help, the young child would do sit-ups on a pillow.*

say, 'Nah, she's fine,' and she was. She'd just swing from bar to bar like a little monkey."

Stefano worked with his infant daughter. When she was just two or three months old, he had her doing sit-ups. He placed a pillow under her body and gently pulled her up. Then, very gently, he'd push her back onto the pillow.

Jennifer was swimming at a very early age, too, and started swinging a tennis racket by the age of three.

## A Permanent Move

Although the Capriatis had moved to America for Jennifer's birth, they had returned to Spain and lived there until Jennifer was four. After Steven, their second child, was born, they moved back to the United States. Stefano thought that his children would get the best education there.

Jennifer's parents had to decide what part of the United States to move to. Denise had grown up in New York. But northern climates are not favored by people interested in tennis. Tennis lovers tend to live in warm, sunny climates like California and Florida. Since the weather is warm there most of the time, tennis can be played throughout the year. With that in mind, the Capriatis chose Florida.

In Florida, Stefano watched little Jennifer as she learned the game of tennis. She never seemed to tire of the sport when she played with her father. And she never tired of it when she hit balls from an automatic server. Stefano must have felt sure that his Jennifer was born for the game of tennis.

And, just like Denise's decision to sit by a pool in Spain, the decision to go back to America was a turning point for young Jennifer's career. With the Capriatis now settled in Lauderhill, Florida, Jennifer continued to learn the game of tennis from her very first coach, her dad.

# 3

# Bring on the Coach
*"Her first serve has now become a weapon."*

Close to the Capriati home, in a place called Holiday Park in Fort Lauderdale, was a tennis coach named Jimmy Evert. He has coached many people but is most famous as the first coach of his own daughter, tennis great, Chris Evert.

Ordinarily, Jimmy Evert had a hard-and-fast rule about the teaching of tennis. He would never take a student under the age of six. But Stefano brought Jennifer to him when she was only five. Stefano must have felt that Jennifer was ready for the next level of instruction.

He was right. When Jimmy Evert first saw Jennifer play, he made an exception to his rule. He took on Jennifer as his student and taught her for the next seven years. Jennifer also got to play with Jimmy's famous daughter, Chris.

Recalling the first time that she hit with Chris, Jennifer says, "I was so nervous. I was so embarrassed because I couldn't hit the ball in the court. I kept thinking, 'She probably thinks I'm so bad.'"

That was the farthest thing from Chris Evert's mind. "I've known Jennifer since she was five years old," said Chris in a 1990 interview, "and I always knew she was a feisty competitor and great athlete."

*As part of her training, young Jennifer often played with Chris, the daughter of Jimmy Evert, who was Jennifer's first professional coach. Jennifer and Chris grew to be close friends.*

## The Evert-Capriati Relationship

In a 1990 *Tennis World* magazine interview, Chris Evert talked about the Jimmy Evert–Jennifer Capriati relationship:

> My dad gave her [Jennifer] lessons every day, and before long she was beating all the other kids pretty badly. Then she graduated to the men club players and started beating them. My sister, Jeanne, also played with her once a week, and I hit with her occasionally....When Jennifer was eight or nine, my dad told me that he hadn't seen anyone with so much talent since I started playing. Dad had coached both of my sisters and seen other girls play, but working with Jennifer was like a second life for him.

And Jimmy Evert had a lot to be excited about. His youngest student wasn't just beating the kids at Holiday Park's tennis courts. She was becoming well known in the world of amateur tennis as well.

## A Fluffy Reward

In 1988, just after her twelfth birthday, Jennifer won the girls' title at the Omega Easter Bowl. That summer she also won the USTA National Girls' Hard Court and Clay Court Championships. But there was one other tournament she desperately wanted to win.

For two years in a row, Jennifer had entered the Rolex Orange Bowl, a tournament held during the Christmas season, and both times she had lost.

There was more than just the "win" riding on this match, however. Jennifer's father had promised her a dog if she won the Orange Bowl. So, for two years, Jennifer had lost not only the competition but also her chance to get a puppy.

By the time Jennifer was ready to try for a third time, Stefano and Denise realized that maybe they had been putting too much pressure on Jennifer. So, just before she entered the Orange Bowl—which she would once again lose—her parents presented her with an early Christmas gift, a cuddly white ball of fluff. Jennifer named her puppy Bianca.

## *Another Coach Is Added*

Bianca was probably a real blessing for Jennifer at that time. Her tennis schedule was making her life more and more hectic as she worked to keep up with her school work and her weekday tennis practices. And now Jennifer had a weekend tennis coach who lived far away. The family had to travel every weekend from their home in southeastern Florida up to Orlando, in east central Florida. There, Jennifer trained and practiced with pro player, Rick Macci, at the Grenlefe Resort and Conference Center.

Was Jennifer's additional coaching a shock to Jimmy Evert? Not really. Most coaches don't expect to be the only expert to work with a particular athlete. Each athlete, no matter what the sport, has strengths and weaknesses. Each coach can have different strengths and weaknesses and approaches as to how to play the game. The Capriatis knew that Jennifer had learned a great deal from Jimmy Evert, but they also knew it was time for her to move on.

*Young Jennifer dreamed for a long time of having a puppy of her own. Finally, just before she was to compete in the Orange Bowl tournament, her parents surprised her with a little white dog that she named Bianca.*

## *Jennifer's World Grows Larger*

In 1989, the Capriatis moved the whole family to Haines City, Florida, which was close to Orlando. Now Jennifer was being coached exclusively by Rick Macci.

By this time, Jennifer's game and her great physical strength were such that she would compete with players who were much older. (In accordance with the United States Tennis Association's regulations, young tennis players compete against people their own age. If they are good enough, they can "play up." That means they compete against older players.)

That's exactly what Jennifer was doing. At 13, she was winning tournaments against 18-year-olds! And she was participating in, and winning, tournaments that brought her a lot farther than the state of Florida.

In 1989, Jennifer won the junior division singles championships at the French and U.S. opens, and the junior doubles of the U.S. Open and Wimbledon championships.

Jennifer Capriati was named *World Tennis* and *Tennis Magazine* Junior Player of the Year and *Tennis Magazine*/Rolex Watch Rookie of the year. She was also recognized by the U.S. Olympic Committee as Athlete of the Year in the Sport of Tennis.

Not only was Jennifer on her "way up," but she also appeared to have reached the top. There were no other players to beat.

## Shaping Up

Despite all the awards, Stefano felt that his daughter's game could improve even more and that her body could be strengthened. That's why he approved of the United States Tennis Association's decision to send Jennifer to Arlington, Virginia, to visit the Sports Medicine Institute. There, she was given a whole series of tests. Body fat, aerobic endurance, and muscle strength, among other skills, were determined. Her agility and speed on the court were also tested. According to Janet Sobel, the physical therapist who gave Jennifer the tests, her scores were excellent.

There was, however, one piece of bad news. Jennifer's right shoulder muscles were weak and needed strengthening. If this condition was not corrected, it could mean the end of Jennifer's tennis career.

Perhaps because of his own past soccer injuries, Stefano recognized the need for just this sort of testing. Jennifer also knew only too well how injuries could cut short a career. Tracy Austin and Andrea Jaeger were young and shining tennis stars much like Jennifer Capriati. Both of them had their careers end quickly because of injuries that they suffered playing tennis.

With Austin's, Jaeger's, and her dad's experiences in her thoughts, Jennifer tackled her exercises vigorously. She did everything that

*Jennifer's great physical strength and endurance have always been among her finest assets.*

was prescribed. In a little more than three months, she improved dramatically. Her coach witnessed the progress, too. "The training and conditioning exercises have enabled Jennifer to spend less time on the court and more time becoming a better all-around athlete. In just three months I've seen her become faster, stronger, more explosive, and more flexible," said Rick Macci.

**The Winning Spirit**

United States Tennis Association coach, Lynne Rolley, noticed other benefits. "Her first serve has now become a weapon.... The off-court conditioning seemed to improve the consistency of her serve over long matches. And her overhead is stronger."

Jennifer returned from her Virginia training a far stronger player. Her serves were clocked at more than 90 miles an hour. Everything was looking up, and Jennifer was ready and willing to turn professional. Unfortunately, there was a hitch. Jennifer was still only 13 years old. The Women's International Tennis Association had strict rules about the age of their professional players. According to them, no one under age 14 could turn pro.

What could Jennifer do? She had no option but simply to wait.

# 4

# Turning Pro
*"When I hear the crowd getting into it, I really get into it, too"*

Jennifer didn't have to wait too long to get a knock on the door. But it wasn't from the professional women's tennis organizations...yet.

The knocks came from a variety of big American companies who wanted Jennifer to endorse their products.

## Endorsing Company Products

When someone agrees to endorse a company's product, it means that he or she has to be available for commercials and personal appearances and also has to use the product. In exchange, the person doing the endorsing receives a large salary.

It all sounds wonderful, but it takes a lot of time out from training and playing. And, for

Jennifer sits in the stands watching the action at one of her first pro tournaments. With her is her brother, Steven, and behind her on the right is her father, Stefano.

**The Winning Spirit**

someone as young as Jennifer, earning huge sums of money could be hard to handle.

There were a number of reasons so many companies approached Jennifer Capriati.

First, she was a great tennis player, and people felt certain that she had a long career ahead of her.

Secondly, she had started more and more to appear in the national tennis spotlight. People knew she was an engaging, bubbly teenager. Except for her growing fame and her incredible tennis talent, she was very much like young American girls all over the country. She loved being with her friends, going to the mall, playing with her dog, listening to music, and watching movies. She was the perfect person to advertise a whole host of products.

Finally, add the fact that Jennifer was one of the only American teenage tennis stars around. Tracy Austin and Andrea Jaeger were no longer playing tennis. Companies that look for young female athletes that other kids can relate to were longing for someone just like Jennifer.

The Capriatis turned to the Evert family for guidance about business. Chris's brother, John Evert, at International Management Group, became Jennifer's manager. It was his job to work with the Capriatis to make sure that Jennifer was not overloaded with work endorsing products. John Evert said, "The last thing we want to do is tie her up to a lot of endorsements where she has to give up a lot of days."

No one wanted Jennifer exhausted before she even got onto the courts. She limited her endorsements to Diadora, an Italian sportswear company, Prince rackets, and Oil of Olay skin products. For these endorsements, Jennifer would receive millions of dollars.

## Making History

Jennifer was certainly headed for the pro tennis courts. When she was just a few weeks shy of her fourteenth birthday, the Women's International Tennis Association allowed Jennifer to enter the Virginia Slims of Florida. That meant Jennifer Capriati was officially a pro.

Reporters quickly swarmed the Boca Raton area, where Jennifer played her first pro match. Before this, she had stayed out of the public eye by practicing at private locations. She got plenty of rest. And she kept up with her school work. The Palmer Academy sent assignments to her—being a pro didn't change Jennifer's commitment to school work.

On the day of the match, Jennifer was with her family in the home of the one friend who could totally sympathize with her...Chris Evert. Even though Chris was away, her faith in Jennifer must have been felt, for Jennifer played magnificently.

Jennifer was the winner of her first pro match. On March 6, 1990, she defeated 10-year pro veteran Mary Lou Daniels. Then she went on to defeat Claudia Porwik, Nathalie Tauziat, Helena Sukova, and Laura Gildemeister before finally losing to Gabriela Sabatini.

Jennifer had made history! She was the youngest player ever to reach the finals of a women's tennis tournament. She had amazed the public with her pounding baseline shots

*Jennifer concentrates on a shot during the 1990 Virginia Slims tournament. She went on to make history by being the youngest player to ever reach the finals in a women's pro match.*

and her seemingly boundless energy. Gabriela Sabatini later commented, "I had to play my best tennis to beat her. She should be in the top ten very soon."

And Jennifer loved every minute of it.

"When I hear the crowd getting into it, I really get into it, too" she said. And on that

*The Winning Spirit*

Sunday, part of the crowd *really* got into it. A large group of her close friends from Palmer Academy came to Boca Raton to see her play.

With colorful poster cards, they assembled the message G-O J-E-N-N-I-F-E-R.

Even after all the attention she gets from the press, Jennifer values her friends more than ever. "They don't treat me any different," she says. "I'm just the same old Jennifer to them."

As a pro, Jennifer has always remembered her fans. After every match, she signs as many autographs as she can.

## The Life of a Pro

In some ways, "the same old Jennifer" has her days structured just as tightly as before she turned pro. She rises early and attends school from 7:00 A.M. until 11:00 A.M. Then she practices tennis for several hours. After that, it's back to school in the evening. She winds up her day by relaxing to music or watching a movie, but only after a strenuous and lengthy workout at the gym.

Jennifer must also fit travel into this rigorous schedule. As a pro, she plays in tennis tournaments all over the world.

After her debut in Boca Raton, Jennifer became singles champion in Puerto Rico. She made it to the semifinals at the French Open and to the quarterfinals in Montreal, Canada, and Italy. In 1990 alone, Jennifer earned more than a quarter of a million dollars in prize money. Out of 53 matches played, she won 42.

Also in that year, she was on the cover of *Newsweek* magazine and *Sports Illustrated* and was the subject of numerous articles in many other publications.

## Keeping Life in Focus

Just in case the glory and all the endorsement money go to her head, Jennifer's mom is always there, ready to give her daughter sound advice. "It's a little scary," Denise says. "It's all happening so fast. Every day it's something

Jennifer proudly raises the trophy she won after defeating Monica Seles in the Pathmark Classic in 1991.

*Jennifer took some time out during a recent visit to New York to help three-year-old Benjamin Glicksberg with his forehand. Staying close to her fans helps Jennifer keep her success and fame in perspective.*

new. I know that Jennifer is really hot, but she's still a teenager. But I also have a lot of confidence in her. She's bright, and she's going to make the right decisions. She's going to make some wrong ones, too, but that's the only way she'll learn.

**The Winning Spirit**

"I look at all the wonderful things happening to Jennifer, but you have to be realistic.... I told Jennifer, 'Listen, if something happens, God forbid, these people won't even recognize you next year. So just keep that in your head.' Unfortunately, that's the way life is. It's tough, and I want her to realize it's not all strawberries and cream."

Tennis legend Billie Jean King also had words of warning for Jennifer. "It's really fun for me to see somebody her age and how well she handles things," said King in an interview. "But sophomore year [on the pro circuit] is the dangerous one. The first year, everything is new, and nobody really has the book on you. But it gets tougher after that. The one thing I've stressed to Jennifer is just to keep the love of the game very close to your heart."

# 5

## *Star-Spangled Summer*

***"I got the chance to do what so many other great athletes had done, to stand up there."***

At the Olympic Village in August of 1992, it was easy for Jennifer to keep the love of the game very close to her heart. She was surrounded by the world's top athletes from many sports. They represented countries from around the globe. Like Jennifer, they were dedicated to excellence. Even though these people spoke different languages, there was a common, unspoken language—their love for the game they played.

The atmosphere was also far different from anything Jennifer had ever experienced. Here she was surrounded by many people close to her own age who were also accomplished athletes. They had all been in the spotlight, too. None of them put pressure on her to sign autographs. They didn't hang onto her every word the way Jennifer's fans had a tendency to do back home in the United States.

"I love my fans and stuff," Jennifer once explained in an interview, "but you just can't [sign autographs for everyone]. I feel bad because people say, 'Oh, you're not doing anything,' but they don't understand that I can't be everything to everyone.

"They expect me to do all this stuff because I did it last year. But this year it's a little different. Sometimes I need to be by myself and just be able to go and watch a match privately without having to sign autographs or talk to anyone."

## Independence for Jennifer

Prior to Jennifer's Olympic competitions, Denise and Stefano tried to change things for their daughter. After the Tokyo disaster, Stefano had told reporters, "She didn't say to me that she hates me or her coach, and she didn't say she hates tennis...she just had moments where she was not a happy camper."

Stefano learned that he had to give Jennifer a little more time on her own. Like any teenager, she wanted a sense of independence. So for Christmas of 1991, the Capriatis allowed Jennifer to go to Mexico to stay with a girlfriend and her family. Jennifer had never traveled on

*Being part of the American team and winning the gold at the Barcelona Olympics in 1992 was one of the greatest thrills of Jennifer's life.*

her own before. It was something she had wanted to experience.

They also let Jennifer have more control over her tennis schedule. And Stefano has stopped overseeing how his daughter is coached. Plus Jennifer now regularly holds press conferences on her own.

Stefano added, "Right now she needs me as a father, not as a coach. This way we can keep them separate.

"Jenny has been our teacher, too. She makes mistakes, we make mistakes, and the family learns from the mistakes. And we try not to make a big deal of it."

Because her family was listening to her concerns, Jennifer was happier and more relaxed as she trained for the Olympics.

## Playing for the Gold

For two weeks, Jennifer competed in the singles tennis competition, and she was playing well. Instead of barreling through a game, she was taking her own time. When the rules allowed, she stopped and toweled off. Things were going well on the court, and Jennifer was winning. She reached the semifinals and won against Spain's own Arantxa Sánchez-Vicario.

Jennifer was now going to compete with Steffi Graf. Steffi, representing Germany, was the one world-champion player Jennifer had never beaten.

Would Jennifer have the stamina and the confidence to beat her?

If Jennifer could win, it would mean a gold medal for her country. It would mean an end to her year of continual losses. And it would be an added bit of joy for her parents. After all, Spain was the country where they had met 20 years before.

Steffi won the first set, with a score of 6-3. Looking back on that game, Jennifer says that she wasn't at all discouraged by her loss. "It actually gave me confidence. If I was giving her a hard time on her serve, it put a little more pressure on her."

The two young women readied themselves for the next set. Steffi blew rapidly on her fingers before each serve. Jennifer nervously bit on her towel each time she wiped off. After much hard work, Jennifer won the second set, with a score of 6-3.

The final set was now under way with the score 4-5, and Jennifer was leading. But a set can be won only if there is a two-point spread. That meant Jennifer still had to win one more game against one of the best.

Jennifer and Steffi had time out. Jennifer's old friend, former tennis star Chris Evert, was the sports commentator. At that moment, Chris recalled another game when Jennifer was close to winning against a tough competitor but wound up losing.

"If that ever happens again," Chris reported Jennifer saying with determination, "I'm going to play aggressively."

It was Jennifer's serve. Steffi stood ready. They used ground strokes...back and forth, back and forth, with each of them playing their best. Then Steffi hit the ball out of bounds. Jennifer was ahead 15-0. Jennifer served and

*The Winning Spirit*

Jennifer (left) soaks in the cheers as she stands with her Olympic competitors. From left to right: Jennifer Capriati, Steffi Graf, Arantxa Sánchez-Vicario, and Mary Jo Fernandez.

aced the ball. Jennifer was now ahead 30-0. But Steffi returned a shot far to the right and behind Jennifer. Jennifer could not return it. Steffi was gaining. The score was 30-15 as Jennifer served again.

"Yes!" Jennifer's fans roared from the stands. Steffi Graf hit the ball out of bounds. Jennifer had scored 40. 40-15 was the new

*The Winning Spirit*

*Because she still has so many years ahead of her, Jennifer has the entire world of tennis eagerly waiting to see her reach new heights.*

score. Jennifer needed just one point to win the set, the match, and the gold!

She circled round, bounced the ball, once, twice, three times. She served. Steffi returned. Each one returned the other's shot...until WONK! Steffi Graf's return barreled low and into the net.

The winner: Jennifer Capriati—youngest American to win the gold medal in tennis. Sixteen-year-old Jennifer beamed. She threw a big kiss to the crowd, exactly where her mom, dad, brother, and coach—Manuel Santana— were sitting.

Wearing her official United States tennis outfit, Jennifer walked proudly up onto the highest pedestal, reserved for the first-place winner. With the American flag swaying high over her head, Jennifer accepted the gold medal for the United States of America.

"I've been watching all the other Americans go up there, and I'd say, 'Gee, I bet that would be cool to be up there,'" said Jennifer. "I got the chance to do what so many other great athletes had done, to stand up there."

Yes, Jennifer stood up there because she had won the Olympics, but she was also on that pedestal because, for a lifetime, she had worked hard and with true determination.

And, as "The Star-Spangled Banner" began to play, Jennifer Capriati, teenage tennis great, wept tears of joy.

# Glossary

**ace** To win a point by serving a ball so fast and so well that the other player cannot possibly return it.
**baseline** The back line located at each end of the tennis court.
**debut** A first appearance.
**endorse** To approve of something; in advertising, to publicly proclaim a product's value.
**love** No score; zero.
**open** A tournament in which both amateurs and professionals may compete.
**quarterfinals** The matches in the round before the semifinal round of a tournament.
**semifinals** The matches in the round before the final round of a tournament.
**set** The number of games played for someone to be declared a winner.

# For Further Reading

Bracken, Charles. *Tennis: Play Like a Pro.* Mahwah, NJ: Troll, 1990.
Gutman, Bill. *Jennifer Capriati, Teenage Tennis Star.* Brookfield, CT: Millbrook, 1993.
Morrissette, Mikki. *Jennifer Capriati.* Boston: Little, Brown and Company, 1991.
White, Ellen. *Jennifer Capriati.* New York: Scholastic, 1991.

# *Index*

Austin, Tracy, 24, 29
Australian Open, 6

Capriati, Denise (mother), 9, 13–15, 17, 21, 33, 38
Capriati, Jennifer
  birth, 15
  company endorsements, 27–29
  honors, 23
  seasonal statistics, 6, 33
  titles, 20, 23, 33
  training, 12, 21, 24–26, 33
  turning pro, 30
Capriati, Stefano (father), 9, 14–15, 16, 17, 21, 24, 28, 38, 40
Capriati, Steven (brother), 9, 17, 28
Clay Court competition, 20

Daniels, Mary Lou, 30
Diadora, 29

Evert, Chris, 9, 18, 19, 20, 29, 30, 41, 42
Evert, Jeanne, 20
Evert, Jimmy, 9, 19, 20, 22
Evert, John, 29

Fernandez, Mary Jo, 43
French Open, 23, 33

Gildemeister, Laura, 30
Graf, Steffi, 40–43, 45
Gullikson, Tom, 11

Haines City, Florida, 23
Holiday Park, 18, 20
*100 Rifles*, 14

International Management Group, 29

Jaeger, Andrea, 24, 29

King, Billie Jean, 36

*Last Run, The*, 14
Lauderhill, Florida, 17
Lipton International Players Championships, 9, 11

Macci, Rick, 21, 23, 25

Navratilova, Martina, 5, 6
*Newsweek* magazine, 33

Oil of Olay, 29
Olympic Committee, U.S., 23
Olympic Games (1992), 5, 6, 12, 37–38, 39, 40–43, 45
Omega Easter Bowl, 20

**47**

Palmer Academy, 6, 30, 32
Pan Pacific Open, 6
Pathmark Classic, 34
*Patton*, 14
Porwik, Claudia, 30
Prince rackets, 29

Rolex Orange Bowl, 21, 22
Rolley, Lynne, 26

Sabatini, Gabriela, 6, 30, 31
Sánchez-Vicario, Arantxa, 40, 43
Santana, Manuel, 12, 45
Seles, Monica, 9, 11, 34
Slozil, Pavel, 11
Sobel, Janet, 24
*Sports Illustrated* magazine, 33

Sports Medicine Institute, 24
Sukova, Helena, 30

Tauziat, Nathalie, 30
*Tennis Magazine*, 23
Tokyo, Japan, 6

United States Tennis Association, 24, 26
U.S. Open, 23
USTA National Girls' Hard Court competition, 20

Virginia Slims tournament, 30

Wimbledon, 5, 23
Women's International Tennis Association, 26, 30
*World Tennis* magazine, 23

**Photo Credits:**
Cover: ©Manuela Dupont/Gamma Liaison; p. 4: AP/Wide World Photos; p. 7: AP/Wide World Photos; p. 10: ©Jimmy Bolcina/Gamma Liaison; p. 25: ©Roland Garros/Gamma Liaison; p. 28: AP/Wide World Photos; p. 31: AP/Wide World Photos; p. 32: ©Manuela Dupont/Gamma Liaison; p. 34: AP/Wide World Photos; p. 35: AP/Wide World Photos; p. 39: Gamma Liaison; pp. 42–43: Gamma Liaison; p. 44: AP/Wide World Photos.

Illustrations by Dick Smolinski.